30-Day Journey

with St. Hildegard of Bingen

30-Day Journey

with St. Hildegard of Bingen

Compiled and Edited by Shanon Sterringer

Fortress Press

Minneapolis

30-DAY JOURNEY WITH ST. HILDEGARD OF BINGEN

Cover design: Paul Soupiset
Interior design: Paul Soupiset
Typesetting: Jessica Ess, Hillspring Books

Print ISBN: 978-1-5064-5056-8
eBook ISBN: 978-1-5064-5057-5

The paper used in this publication meets the mini-
mum requirements of American National Standard
for Information Sciences — Permanence of Paper for
Printed Library Materials, ANSI Z329.48-1984.

Manufactured in the U.S.A.

Contents

In the Serene Light I saw and heard a voice saying to you: Your mind is like a flood of water, and like a net not properly spread to catch the prey, because you wish those things to be done that you desire or command, but sometimes it does not happen so. But observe that the plowman first turns over the earth, and, afterward, harrows it. Only then does he plant his seeds.

—Letter from Hildegard to an Abbot

Introduction

Hildegard of Bingen was born in 1098 CE to Hildebert and Mecthilde in Niederhosenbach or possibly Bermersheim, Germany. Most of the biographical information on Hildegard is recorded in her *Vita* (medieval biography), which was composed over several years by at least five scholars, including Hildegard herself. According to her *Vita*, at the age of eight years old Hildegard was tithed as an anchorite to the Benedictine monastery at Disibodenberg under the care of Jutta of Sponheim, a recluse also born of nobility. Hildegard may not have actually entered the monastery until she took her vows as a young teenager, around the year 1115 CE.

From a very young age she was gifted with visions. She studied sacred Scriptures and theology. Hildegard learned to preach and came to master the art of building and administering a monastery at Rupertsberg, which would later expand to a second monastery across the Rhine River in Eibingen. In 1136 CE Jutta died, and Hildegard was named the new *magistra* of her community. In 1141 CE, at the age of forty-three, Hildegard experienced a vision of the "Living Light," which commanded her to put into writing the words and images that would be revealed to her. The Living Light for Hildegard is the divine energy source from which emerges all that exists. Her initial writings were well received by the hierarchy, and in 1148 CE Pope Eugenius III publicly read excerpts from her work at the Synod of Trier. It was determined that her writings were in fact coming from a divine source, and she was given permission to write down all that the Living Light revealed to her. It was from her connection to the Living Light that Hildegard received her visions and spiritual authority. With the help of Volmar (a Benedictine priest/monk who served as her secretary, confessor, and closest friend for over sixty years) and one of her dearly beloved nuns, Richardis of Stade, she completed her first theological book, *Scivias*, which was published in 1151 CE.

As Hildegard's reputation grew, so did the number of women (wealthy and well-educated) seeking entry into her religious community. The influx of newly vowed religious created a need for larger quarters. Soon after the synod granted Hildegard permission to write theology, she received a vision instructing her to move her sisters out of Disibodenberg to their own monastery, where they would be free, to some extent, from the immediate control of the abbot and the male hierarchy. With some difficulty, and courageous effort, she sought and received permission from the abbot and the archbishop of Mainz to move her sisters to their own monastery. The margravine of Stade (the mother of Richardis) endowed Hildegard's convent with a piece of land. Hildegard began construction immediately, and the convent chapel at Rupertsberg was blessed by Heinrich, archbishop of Mainz, in 1152 CE.

Over the next several years, Hildegard was deeply engaged in writing, composing, healing, preaching, and leading her sisters to grow in light and love by embracing the Benedictine Rule. She completed her second theological work, *Liber Vitae Meritorum* (The Book of the Rewards of Life), in the early 1160s and her third theological work, *Liber Divinorum Operum* (Book of Divine Works), in the years to follow. During this time, Hildegard suffered from illness and often found herself bedridden for months at a time, though this did not hinder her ministry. In 1158 CE, she received permission to go on a series of four preaching tours. Her homilies were collected and preserved.

In 1165 CE, Hildegard founded a second monastery at Eibingen, across the Rhine River from Rupertsberg. While the monastery building itself no longer exits, today a parish church stands on the property housing Hildegard's reliquary, which is believed to include her heart and tongue. The new cloistered Benedictine Abbey of St. Hildegard was built in 1904 at the top of a hill in Eibingen overlooking the parish church.

Hildegard wrote two works on the natural world and herbal healing, *Physica* and *Causae et Curae*; composed over seventy liturgical hymns; wrote the first known morality play, *Ordo Virtutum*; wrote several minor works and two hagiographies; contributed to her own *Vita*; created her own language; and produced visual pieces of art (miniatures) to accompany several of her visions. Throughout her life, Hildegard corresponded with many high-ranking men and women, civil and religious, including kings and popes. Her collection of letters uniquely captures her spirit. The daily excerpts for this book were chosen from her personal letters. The translations in this volume and the dating of the letters are the work of Joseph L Baird and Radd K. Ehrman in their three-volume set *The Letters of St. Hildegard*, published between the years 1994 and 2004.

Outside of Germany, Hildegard has been virtually unknown for almost eight hundred years. Her works were rediscovered in the mid-twentieth century. It has taken scholars decades to digest and translate the *summa* that has been preserved. The depth of her work is still being explored and studied by scholars, theologians, artists, musicians, feminists, and ecologists. In 2012, Pope Benedict XVI canonized Hildegard of Bingen a saint and named her a doctor of the church.

Hildegard offers women and men today an example of extraordinary leadership. She was a woman who embraced her time and yet can properly be called a woman ahead of her time. Her ecological message, which reflects a deep respect for the sanctity of the environment and the interconnectedness of all creation, has much to teach us regarding our divinely ordered place within the cosmos. Hildegard's theological concept of *viriditas*, or greening power, which she believed was the life force that animates the entire created world, has the power to heal the mind, body, and spirit.

Hildegard stood strong in the midst of raging storms, and she never wavered in speaking, with the voice of a prophet, what she believed was truth. She led with confidence and integrity. St. Hildegard of Bingen knew who she was and what she was being called to do. Nothing prevented her from following the voice of the Living Light. Her letters give us a unique glimpse into her personality and complex thought. May they be a source of inspiration for you during this thirty-day journey.

Days 1-30

Remain in the garden where you presently are until your mind has fewer flaws, and until, as far as possible, you bring to perfection all the good things you are gathering into the bosom of your mind in that community where you now reside. Restrain yourself with the bridle of fear of the Lord so that you may avoid the dangerous paths. Get a grip on yourself until you see better times, and you will live.

—*Letter from Hildegard to a Certain Person*

Hildegard wrote hundreds of letters to women and men in all walks of life, including those in positions of authority and leadership, secular and religious. Her letters offer practical advice, spiritual direction, and at times challenging critiques to help the recipient, whether an individual or community, grow in mind, body, and spirit. Many of her letters are creatively written in the genre of allegory or metaphor, such as the image of a garden. The recipient of this letter is unknown. It is believed to have been written before the year 1170 CE.

Reflection

Each of us has different gifts and dreams of how to use them, but our lives push and pull us in many directions. It's easy to feel trapped and restricted by the demands of the roles we fill. From the time she was tithed as a child, Hildegard spent her life (she lived to be eighty-one years old) as a Benedictine sister, shut off from the rest of the world. She was far too gifted, however, to remain hidden from the world. She learned to balance her solitary lifestyle, which was steeped in prayer, meditation, gardening, music, and the expectations of religious life, with her vocation to be engaged with the world through preaching, writing, traveling, healing, and even politics. Hildegard did not allow her personal flaws, or the confines of a monastery, to keep her from blooming and producing fruit for the world to enjoy. She used the imperfect space and circumstances she had been given as a garden to grow in her own perfection. How would you describe the garden in which you presently reside? How can you grow from its challenges?

The Shadow of God's mysteries says: The wind blows, the air shifts, and clouds become so intermingled that sometimes they are stormy, sometimes black, sometimes white, and sometimes luminous. And you are just that, O knight of God. For sometimes you have worldly sadness like the blowing wind, and sometimes you are caught up in the pleasure that the devil lays down as a trap like the shifting air, and sometimes you are morally astray like the mingling clouds, so that sometimes your morals are squalid storms, sometimes terrified in darkness, sometimes sweet in whiteness, sometimes wholesome in luminosity.

—*Letter from Hildegard to the Monk Heinrich*

The following excerpt is from a letter Hildegard wrote to a monk named Heinrich. Heinrich's letter was one of great praise for Hildegard's holiness. He drew on images from the sacred Scriptures to describe her virtue and spiritual beauty. Expressing his belief that God had bestowed special graces on Hildegard, Heinrich requested that she pray for him. Hildegard responds with a challenge to the monk to strive for holiness by properly repenting in order to be restored to a state of purity. The corresponding letters are believed to have been written before the year 1170 CE.

Reflection

Life is in a constant state of flux, and storms rise without warning. In our ever-changing realities, we need to stay grounded and focused on the presence of the Living Light, which seeks to redeem us. The Living Light for St. Hildegard is the primordial life source through which all that exists came into being. It is the source that sustains all of creation, and it is the means by which the mysteries of the universe are revealed. Where have you felt storms rising recently? As you experience the challenges of your day, focus on the places and moments where you can experience the presence of the Living Light.

And I heard a voice saying of you: A man who toils with plow and oxen in arid land says to himself: I cannot endure this difficult labor because it is too hard for me. And so he goes into the desert [cf. Luke 11:24], where delicate flowers grow uncultivated by human effort, but which are being suffocated by unwholesome weeds. And again he says to himself: I will put aside my plow, and pull up these useless weeds. What is the good in this? Now, O man, consider who is better: the one toiling in the earth with a useful plow, or the one who pulls up useless weeds growing amid the flowers. I saw also that this matter you are asking about is unwholesome for you. Therefore, stay in your position with your hand to the plow.

—*Letter from Hildegard to the Abbot Withelo*

Hildegard's reputation as a religious sage had begun to spread while she was still under the care of Jutta of Sponheim, and her advice was widely sought after. In time it would lead to her being nicknamed the "Sybil of the Rhine." This excerpt is a response to a letter an abbot named Withelo wrote to Hildegard seeking advice on a decision regarding his position at a monastery. Withelo's original letter no longer exists. The date for Hildegard's response is believed to be earlier than 1153 CE.

Reflection

It is not uncommon to find ourselves at a place on our journey where the life choices we have made—our career, our family, and even our spirituality—no longer seem to make sense. Some call this a midlife crisis while others refer to it as a spiritual awakening. Like Withelo, we may find ourselves discerning a call to an entirely new place, or it may be that we are called to remain in the same place but with a new attitude. This excerpt from Hildegard challenges us to take an honest look at what is motivating our restlessness. Is it a genuine spiritual call propelling me out into the desert, or am I fleeing because of my unwillingness to endure the difficult labor necessary for authentic transformation? Discernment is an invitation to take an honest look at your life to determine if the tasks you are engaged in are truly wholesome for you.

The Breath of the Spirit of God says: God covers the tree. He loves it in the wintertime, and He brings forth an abundance of flowers from it in the summer, taking away every disease that might cause it to wither. The pollution characteristic of other waters is cleansed by the river of water that springs out of a rock in the East. This river runs swiftly, and it is more salutary than other waters since it is free from filth. This applies to those people to whom God grants the day of prosperity and the glowing dawn of honor.

—*Letter from Hildegard to Bertha,*
Queen of the Greeks

Hildegard wrote letters not only to religious leaders but also to secular leaders, including kings and queens. She was a gifted politician, and her advice was highly sought, at times even by the Holy Roman emperor Barbarossa. It was Hildegard's political connections that ensured the safety of her monasteries during times of unrest. This excerpt is from a letter written to Bertha of Sulzbach, also known as Eastern Empress Irene, following her marriage to Eastern Emperor Manuel I in 1146 CE. The letter is believed to have been written between 1146 and 1160 CE.

Reflection

During challenging times in our lives and our world, we can feel alone and hurt without hope of renewal. Hildegard believed that even in the midst of a dark and fallen world, the Living Light continues to protect and restore us if we choose to follow the path of love. In this passage, Hildegard describes God's spirit offering protection and renewal to the world through the "river of water that springs out of a rock in the East." This river, pouring out from God's love, is the water of life, which can restore creation and those within it to a place of abundance. Each one of us has the power to choose prosperity instead of filth and disease, simply by engaging in everyday acts of love and gratitude. As you go about your day, look for opportunities to act out of love rather than fear and pain.

Listen now to a wise man's parable: A certain man wanted to dig a cave, but while he was working with wood and iron, fire burst forth from a rock he had dug into. And the result was that this place could in no way be penetrated. Nevertheless, he took note of the location of the place, and with great exertion he dug other tunnels into it. And then the man said in his heart: "I have toiled strenuously, but he who comes after me will have easier labor, because he will find everything already prepared for him." Surely this man will be praised by his lord. . . . For whoever has labored first is preeminent over the one who succeeds him. Indeed, the Maker of the world undertook creation first, and thus set the example for His servants to labor after His fashion. . . . O daughter of God, keep a close watch over the plot of land within you so that it will not wither. . . . Be like fertile earth that is watered often with seasonable rain, so that you may produce good and delectable herbs.

—*Letter from Hildegard to the Abbess*

The following parable is in part a response to a letter Hildegard received from an abbess sometime between 1163 and 1173 CE. The abbess appealed to the biblical story of the Canaanite woman in Matthew 15:27, who desired to receive even the "crumbs that fall from their master's table" as an

Reflection

For Hildegard, humility is the queen of all the virtues. While we long for affirmation and success, it is through acts of humble service, acts that are not always recognized, that we become most fully connected to the Living Light. A handful of people in this generation will be called to become world-renowned leaders making contributions that overtly alter human history. The majority, however, are called to change our world by engaging in daily acts of love and peace in our communities and families. Most of us will be unknown, like the man who wanted to dig a cave in the parable. We may toil and labor without the satisfaction of recognition or even an opportunity to enjoy the fruits of our labor. Yet we can change our world when we embrace the task to make the "plot of land" we have been given a bit sweeter and more fertile for those who will come after us. In what ways are you laboring to prepare the soil entrusted to you?

image of her own desire to receive "crumbs" from Hildegard's table. Having been deeply rooted in the biblical tradition, Hildegard often used parables to convey her message.

The Living Light says: Dry sand is useless, and earth that is too much broken up with the plow will not yield good fruit because it was plowed beyond measure. And dry, rocky ground brings forth only thorns and useless weeds. In the same way, inappropriate abstinence, immoderate and out of proportion, does harm to the fleshy body, for, not receiving the viridity of proper nourishment, it withers away.

—*Letter from Hildegard to Jutta, a Lay Sister*

This excerpt is from a letter written to a lay sister named Jutta. It is believed the letter was written soon after Hildegard moved her sisters out of Disibodenberg to Rupertsberg, sometime between 1153 and 1157 CE. Interestingly, the recipient of this letter is named Jutta, which was the first name of the woman Hildegard was tithed to at Disibodenberg. Jutta of Sponheim (Hildegard's spiritual mother) died in 1136 CE, most likely from complications that resulted from extreme adherence to the Benedictine Rule, including corporal mortification.

Reflection

We are whole beings—mind, body, and spirit—created in the image of God, the *imago Dei*. In our attempt to grow closer to God, we sometimes forget how important it is to not only nourish our spiritual lives with prayers and meditation and our minds with education and positive experiences, but also nourish our bodies. Hildegard believed that "the body is a temple of the Holy Spirit," and so proper care of the body, including physical care, was foundational to her theology. Extreme and immoderate forms of abstinence and penance were common in Hildegard's world, but she often advised a more moderate approach to spiritual practice that cared for the body as well as the soul. When we honor the sanctity of our own bodies, we are honoring God. How can you honor your body today to facilitate healing and wholeness?

Your mind is like a snow cloud, which rises above an airy cloud in which the sun radiates, and sometimes it is like a windy cloud that brings storms. The snow cloud is the weariness of an unstable mind. The airy cloud, however, indicates unsullied knowledge acquired with the patience of faith. But the windy cloud brings the disturbance of great distress found in unquiet minds. Now, learn that the snow cloud is full of air that is neither cold nor hot: wholesome herbs cannot grow from it. The pure air, on the other hand, bestows dew, stable temperature, and rain: vegetation and flowers grow from it. But the windy cloud is full of northern air: from it, all viridity withers, and flowers fall. Now flee these things, and remain steadfast in the pure air.

—*Letter from Hildegard to the Abbot*

Hildegard's reputation as a holy woman spread widely during her lifetime, and clerics often wrote to her for spiritual direction. The abbot addressed in this letter had personally encountered Hildegard and expresses high praise for her holiness. He is in search of words of affirmation and encouragement in the midst of life's storms. This exchange is believed to have been written sometime before 1173 CE.

Reflection

Through our experience of storms in our lives—in our jobs, family, community, church, school, and so on—we discover the grace of our personal strength to overcome chaos and adversity. Hildegard encourages us to find a quiet place, away from the storm, to be still and focused. In this quiet place, name the storms that are raging in your life right now. Bringing an awareness to the anxiety you may be feeling, use your breath to transform it into peace. As you breathe in the pure air of Divine Source (light and love), breathe out (let go) of fear and anxiety. Breathe in and breathe out. This storm too shall pass.

The Light which fully lives says: You, O human being, hear: There was a certain valley that sometimes dried up and sometimes burst forth in flowers. It did not, however, consistently produce wholesome plants, and though it was beautiful for people to see, it was not very useful for sustenance. So it is with your mind. For when you look into yourself and think that you are not strong in good conscience, you immediately dry up, as if you have no hope. But afterward, your mind rises up like the mountain of myrrh and incense [cf. Cant 4.6], rising up in fear, as if you were dead, and, wrestling with yourself, trembling, you flourish again.

—*Letter from Hildegard to Countess Oda of Eberstein*

Hildegard was born into nobility and was comfortable corresponding with German nobles, women and men. As was her style, Hildegard encourages Countess Oda of Eberstein to live by the order of virtue, even at the times when life looks bleak. This letter to the countess is believed to have been written around 1153–1154 CE.

Reflection

Our spiritual journey, like the seasons, is marked by ongoing, and at times unpredictable, change. We are in a consistent cycle moving from life to death. Finding ourselves in a season of drought, we feel intimately the loss of our viridity—our energy and ability to grow. It is easy to become overwhelmed by doubt, sadness, and confusion. Yet, these dry experiences are an integral part of the growing process. They provide an opportunity to restore our greenness (*viriditas* as Hildegard would call it). What season of your spiritual journey are you experiencing right now? Whether feast or famine, as you move through this place on your journey, take a moment to imagine how your current experience can facilitate spiritual growth.

In the Serene Light I saw and heard a voice saying to you: Your mind is like a flood of water, and like a net not properly spread to catch the prey, because you wish those things to be done that you desire or command, but sometimes it does not happen so. But observe that the plowman first turns over the earth, and, afterward, harrows it. Only then does he plant his seeds.

—*Letter from Hildegard to an Abbot*

Hildegard's letters served to advise many abbots and abbesses through practical advice. The following excerpt, believed to have been written before 1170 CE, incorporates a number of allegorical images to communicate the importance of patience in the leadership model.

Reflection

We live in a fast-paced world. Everything has to be immediate, often at the expense of personal relationships and quality results. Our busy schedules make it difficult to practice patience. Many of us are simply trying to stay one step ahead of the demands placed upon us. Hildegard also was a very busy woman: a musician, theologian, writer, religious leader, politician, philosopher, mystic, artist, healer, and visionary. She was challenged, as many of us are, to find ways to juggle all of her responsibilities. She practiced patience to keep herself grounded. How often in your own personal life have you approached situations and relationships unfocused and rushed, later to be disappointed by the end results? Finding creative ways to become fully present, to calm the "flood of water" in our minds, helps us be better prepared for the busyness of our daily lives. Focus on practicing patience today. As you go from one thing to the next, take time to consider your words and actions instead of sprinting forward.

You, O man, who are too tired, in the eye of your knowledge, to rein in the pomposity of arrogance among those placed in your bosom, why do you not call back the shipwrecked who cannot rise from the depths without help? And why do you not cut off the root of evil which is choking out the good and beneficial plants of sweet taste and delightful aroma? You are neglecting the King's daughter who was entrusted to you, that is, heavenly Justice herself. You are allowing this King's daughter to be thrown to the ground; her beautiful crown and tunic torn asunder by the crudeness of those hostile people who bark like dogs and who, like chickens trying to sing at night, raise up their ineffectual voices. They are charlatans, crying out, ostensibly, for peace, but, all the while, biting each other in their hearts, like a dog that wags its tail among those known to him, but bites the honorable knight indispensable to the king's household.... But you, O man ... rise up and run quickly to Justice, so that you will not be accused before the great physician of failing to cleanse his sheepfold and of neglecting to anoint his flock with oil.

—*Letter from Hildegard to Pope Anastasius IV*

Reflection

By virtue of our humanity, we each possess an innate dignity because we are created in the image of God. We have been endowed with so many divine gifts, which we are called to share. We have the inherent right to live our lives in accord with God's divine plan for us, while at the same time we must recognize that with these rights come responsibility. When we are in *right relationship* with all that is sacred—God, ourselves, each other, nature—*viriditas* is renewed and restored. List the spiritual, intellectual, or physical gifts you possess. Are these gifts being used to build a better world or has their divine purpose been neglected? Take a moment to consider how you can use these gifts to help those around you.

Hildegard of Bingen was a reformer. She challenged the clergy of her day on their attitudes of arrogance, clericalism, and corruption. She truly believed God had called her, a woman, to rise up to this challenge. She risked her own well-being to embrace her vocation. This letter was written to Pope Anastasius IV soon after she moved her sisters to Rupertsberg, possibly in 1153–1154 CE.

O viriditas digiti Dei
(O, the greenness of God's finger)

O invigorating power of the finger of God,
in which God planted a garden
which shimmers on the heights
like a steadfast column:
You are glorious in the eternal garden of God.
And you, O lofty mountain,
you will never be brought low
by God's judgment.
And yet you stand afar like an exile,
still, you stand not in the power
of the armed man
who would carry you off.
You are glorious in the eternal garden of God.
Glory to the Father and the Son
and the Holy Spirit
You are glorious in the eternal garden of God.

—*Letter from Hildegard to Abbot Kuno*

Hildegard was an extraordinary musician who wrote many hymns and antiphons to a variety of saints. The following is a hymn she wrote in honor of St. Disibod. She sent this hymn as part of a larger letter to the abbot Kuno at Disibodenberg upon his request. This hymn is believed to have been written before 1155 CE.

Reflection

"You are glorious in the eternal garden of God." When we allow ourselves to truly become the person God created us to be, we begin to shine our glorious light. Hildegard believed that the saints were holy not because they were perfect but because they stayed connected to the green life source—*viriditas*—and from this source drew the strength and fortitude to follow the righteous path. Each one of us is called to be a saint, staying connected to God as we live our lives. In what ways, big or small, are you embracing this extraordinary role? Be confident in the value of your own light.

In the True Light I saw and heard a voice saying to you: Take note of the root that flourishes in soil so rocky that it is almost impossible to plow. Still, it produces perfect fruit, good to the taste. You are that soil beaten upon, as you are, by the heavy storms of war and by the evil winds raised up by the devil. Yet you have the victory in your good reputation, and by the formidable strength of your good works, you will remain steadfast.

—Letter from Hildegard to a Certain Person

The theme of gardening, pruning, and planting seeds in properly prepared soil is common in Hildegard's writings. In this particular passage, written before 1170 CE, she acknowledges that the challenges of life can create rocky and hardened soil, yet by the grace of God growth is possible.

Reflection

When was the last time you planted seeds? Maybe you are a gardener and do so frequently, or maybe you have never planted anything. Regardless, each one of us is charged with the task of sowing spiritual seeds. If you are a gardener, you know that the soil in which seeds are sown largely effects the fruit that is produced. Good soil, however, does not necessarily imply perfect soil. Sometimes, good soil has been enriched by sorrow and suffering and on the surface may appear rocky and weathered. Far more important than what the soil appears like on the surface is the depth of space for the roots to grow. Look at the flower that grows through the crack in the concrete. Guided by light, it finds its way through the hard surface. What are some of the life experiences you have had that have left you feeling beaten up and rocky? Consider how these experiences have made room for deep roots and remember that you can and will grow.

In your works and morals I see you as a tree that has great viridity in its leaves. One branch, however, is drying up. And the elements say: We have come to you on account of the blend of your viridity, but storms injure us. These storms are the doubts and the moral vacillation which, on account of your tribulations, cause you to go in circles, like a mill wheel. But let it not be so. Look to the farmland, which is tilled and plowed and fertilized so that it might bring forth much fruit. This is Patience, which produces humidity and viridity in all good works. Patience's house is harsh and bitter, but it gives great rewards and opens the gates of the heavenly kingdom. And so draw Patience to you, and diligently avoid jacinth and the beryl, which do not flash with brilliance; and keep yourself from those flowers that lack the viridity of virtues and therefore quickly wither, for these love you not for the love of penitence but for the discord of disobedience. . . . Therefore, embrace and kiss Patience, and do not put her aside, for you have the potential to wash clean the wounds of men, and therefore set up a ladder into heaven.

—*Letter from Hildegard to Abbot Manegold (?)*

Reflection

It is no secret that our lives are filled with stress. The source of the stress we experience may come from external places, but it is often self-inflicted. We run ourselves around in circles, "like a mill wheel," with no real sense of focus or purpose, and we become spiritually, emotionally, and physically exhausted. It is hard to acknowledge that we may have been investing a substantial amount of our time with "flowers that lack the viridity of virtue" (whether it's our career, friends, hobbies, or sometimes even family). However, it is through this dry, desert experience that we come to fully appreciate our potential. What areas in your life do you feel have a "dry branch" or a stressful situation in need of healing? How might you turn to the virtue of patience as you acknowledge the need for change?

Hildegard is again using allegorical imagery of a garden to advise an abbot, possibly named Manegold, to turn to the virtue of patience as he leads his community. The letter is believed to have been written between 1156 and 1165 CE.

In a true vision I saw a tree with very green branches. In the summer it tried to burst forth in flowers, but, afflicted with weariness, it could not blossom fully. Therefore, I said to it, "I wanted to cause you to bring forth flowers, but you refused." And the summer ceased in its efforts.... I say to you: Take care not to abandon fiery gifts of the Holy Spirit because of the timorous advice of others or because of the discouraging opinion of this world.

—Letter from Hildegard to Radulf, Teacher

In this letter written to a teacher, presumably a layman named Radulf, Hildegard uses an allegorical image of a tree unsuccessfully trying to burst forth in blossoms. She wrote this letter, sometime before 1170 CE, to encourage Radulf to allow the Holy Spirit to empower his work so that he would not grow weary and fail to blossom.

Reflection

The voices of this world are constantly causing us to question, doubt, and even abandon the task our heart has called us to embrace. These voices can successfully discourage us from fulfilling our divine destiny and living as our best selves. How often have you been inspired and excited by a creative idea only to lose motivation when others laughed at or criticized it? We have within us the gifts we need—wisdom, knowledge, understanding, strength—to stand strong against the voices of this world. Imagine yourself as "a tree with very green branches." What creative idea is waiting to burst forth? Pursue your ideas confidently today as you remember your gifts.

He Who Is says: The sun shines and sends forth its rays. And a certain man, a friend of the sun, had a garden in which he desired to plant many herbs and flowers. And the sun, in the fire of its rays, sent heat upon those herbs, and flowers, and the dew and rain gave the moisture of viridity to them. Then from the north a contorted figure with black hair and horrible face came to that garden, but at the same time from the east came a handsome young man with bright shining hair and a comely, pleasant face. And the contorted figure said to the young man: Where have you come from? And he answered: I come from the east to the garden of this wise man, for I greatly desired to come to him. And the contorted figure said, Listen to me: A destructive wind and hail and fire and pestilence will come upon that garden, and will dry it out. But the young man answered: Not so, it will not be so, because I do not wish it, and I will bring forth a pure fountain and will irrigate the garden. . . . And so the crafty figure brought winter into that garden and sought to dry up the herbs and flowers. And that aforementioned young man, caught up in playing his harp, did not see what was happening. But when he did take notice, he called the sun back with a loud sound . . . and brought viridity of summer back into the garden.

—*Letter from Hildegard to Adam, the Abbot*

Reflection

Everyday life experience can be a struggle between light and dark or good and evil. It seems as though we have to stay continuously vigilant. When we become distracted, as the young man in this story was, we become vulnerable to the darkness. So often the darkness that enters our experience is not something that we invite into our lives, but it slowly creeps in and takes over while we are distracted. Consider some of the dark habits or experiences that have slowly crept into your life over the years. How did it happen? Hildegard challenges us to wake up and stay focused throughout our journey. By choosing the awakened path, we allow the "viridity of summer" to return. Choose to be awake and aware and imagine what the return of summer to those dark places might look like.

As was common to her experience, religious men and woman often sought out Hildegard's advice regarding administrative duties. This particular passage, written to an abbot named Adam, is a beautiful exhortation on leadership as a vocation. The date is unclear but the entire collection of correspondence between Hildegard and this abbot seems to have taken place prior to 1166 CE.

In a spiritual vision by which I frequently see, I saw and understood these things. I see this monastery like a cloud suffused with the kind of light that occurs when day becomes dusk, and night approaches. And I see that there are some among you who shine like stars in their good intent, but that there are others who grow weary, overshadowed by fatigue.... I also saw something like a crown with two circles, one above and one below, both filled with angels. And in the middle of this crown the archangel Michael stood like a tower so that these two circles clung to him like two walls. On his breast shone the image of the Son of man.... With his right arm stretched out, he held a shield in his hand. And next to him was a cloud like golden smoke arising from a censer, in which the meritorious prayers and holy works of the congregation shone. And I heard him saying to this congregation: As long as I see the radiance of holiness in you, I will fight for you against the black, flaming spears that I have seen hurled by impious tyrants against your monastery.

—*Letter from Hildegard to the Congregation of Monks*

Reflection

We are not meant to walk alone in our journeys. Hildegard believed that we are accompanied by a community of angels and saints. St. Michael the archangel was particularly important to Hildegard. She trusted in his ongoing presence with her and knew that regardless of the dangers she faced, he and his angels protected her and her monastery. Think of a time when you knew without a doubt that you had the support and help of another person walking alongside you. What did that experience feel like? Encounters like these remind us of our need for community in our physical and spiritual journeys, especially when we face daunting challenges. When we learn to seek the support of those around us, we find the inspiration and courage to continue, especially when we grow weary.

The community of the monks of St. Michael in Siegburg revered Hildegard as their spiritual mother, referring to themselves as her sons. In this letter, written between 1164 and 1170 CE, she appeals to St. Michael the archangel, the patron of the monks' monastery, to protect and guide them.

It is fitting that the rays of the sun should shine upon that root which has been planted in the Holy Spirit, and that a gentle rain should moisten it for a good field which brings forth good fruit flourishes in the sun and the rain and the dew. Therefore, blessed soul, maintain your temple with discretion, so that the fruitfulness with which you embrace God does not wither, because God greatly loves your soul, and He will gather you into His bosom and will receive you into eternal felicity.

—*Letter from Hildegard to a Certain Person*

Little is known about the recipient of this letter. Scholars believe it was written sometime before 1170 CE. Underlying this passage is the biblical theme of the "body as a temple of the Holy Spirit" as it is described in 1 Corinthians 6:19.

Reflection

Your whole being—mind, body, and spirit—is sacred and reveals the presence of the living God. If you are to "flourish in the sun and the rain and the dew," it is not enough to be engaged in a healthy spiritual life. You also need to be concerned with the needs of your mind and body. The soul is an expression of God, so it naturally follows that there needs to be genuine concern for the temple in which God's presence resides. In Hildegard's day, physical acts of penance, such as extreme fasting and flagellation, were common. It is probable Hildegard's spiritual mother, Jutta of Sponheim, died at a young age from the consequences of this extreme spiritual practice. Unfortunately, there are a number of ways people continue to punish themselves through self-inflicted wounds to the mind, body, and spirit today. Check in for a moment with your own temple. Where are you wounded? In response, think of ways you can express care and appreciation for yourself through your thoughts and actions.

He who knows and discerns all creatures, Who rouses them and is watching over them, the Living Eye sees and says, the valleys are complaining against the mountains, and the mountains are falling into the valleys. What does this mean? Subordinates are no longer disciplined by the fear of God, and madness sends them scaling the heights of the mountains to rail at their superiors. And they are too blind to see the error of their evil ways. . . . Purify your eyes so that nothing escapes your notice. Let your mind be watered by the pure fountain so that you may shine with the Sun and imitate the Lamb. This poor little woman trembles because she speaks with the sound of words to so great a magistrate.

—*Letter from Hildegard to Pope Eugenius III*

Hildegard was a politician as well as a spiritual leader. She was intimately connected to the powers of her day. In this letter, written around 1153 CE, Hildegard is writing to Pope Eugenius III out of support for Heinrich, archbishop of Mainz, who had been removed from his office. Heinrich had brought Hildegard's first theological work, *Scivias*, to Pope Eugenius at the Council of Trier and therefore she was loyal to Heinrich.

Reflection

The spiritual journey empowers us to be agents of light and love in our world. Our experiences form us to grow into the person we were created to be. Hildegard was tithed as an anchorite (cloistered nun) when she was a child, yet she developed into a strong, empowered, public woman. She is often labeled a feminist. However, she would not have identified herself with this label, though she certainly cut across the social, religious, and cultural boundaries of her day. Hildegard saw a divine order to all of creation, and in that order she believed she was created for a particular purpose. When she failed to follow her divine call, she often found herself sick and bedridden until she mustered the courage to resume her journey. Looking to Hildegard as a model, consider your particular purpose. Where might you be called to embrace a new role, crossing social, religious, or cultural boundaries, within your community, family, or workplace? Follow her example of courage as you lean into your purpose.

The True Light says these words: There was a flower in a certain valley, but the gardeners came and planted a thorny hedge all around it, and so, in their malice, choked it off, with the leaves all bent down and broken up by winds. Thus that flower lost all its vitality. And still the gardeners paid no attention to it, and did not love it. Instead, they went looking for another flower, but finding only a weed, they cast it aside. Then, they found a delicate, red flower, and turned their thoughts wholly to it. Nevertheless, they did not plant a decorative hedge around it, nor protect it from the bad weather, but simply allowed it to stand without defense. Yet, a certain man came along, and set a protective covering over that flower, so that it would not utterly perish.

—*Letter from Hildegard to a Certain Person*

This letter, written to an anonymous recipient before 1170 CE, employs a common literary technique in Hildegard's writing: the use of allegory. She is demonstrating her understanding of the relationship between the Hebrew and Christian Scriptures culminating in the person of Jesus. This allegorical image is commentary on the "new law" pointing to the kingdom of God not as something external but a reality found within.

Reflection

How do you measure your personal value? Do you look to the material world for validation? Our personal value far exceeds what we do for a living, what name brand of clothing we wear, how attractive we think we are, what neighborhood we live in, or how much money we have in the bank. Our misplaced desires for external goods keep us from appreciating, or even recognizing, the gift of Living Light within. When this happens, our sacred flower, as Hildegard calls our souls and inner worth, can begin to feel choked out and lose its vitality. Acknowledge how often you find yourself looking outward for love, affirmation, and acceptance and remember the value that already exists within.

Listen now: a king sat on his throne, surrounded by lofty columns bedecked with fine ornaments and set on bases of ivory. And these columns displayed the king's vestments proudly to all. Then it pleased the king to lift up a small feather from the ground, and commanded it to fly, as he himself wished. Yet a feather does not fly of its own accord, but the air bears it along. And I, like the feather, am not endowed with great powers or human education, nor do I even have good health, but I rely wholly on God's help.

—*Letter from Hildegard to Odo of Paris*

In an early set of correspondence, possibly around 1148-1149 CE, Professor Odo of the University of Paris wrote to Hildegard asking for her to clarify a philosophical question regarding the nature of God as both paternal and divine. Hildegard, appealing to the wisdom infused in her by the Living Light, begins her response with the following story.

Reflection

Imagine for a moment you are a feather floating about as the wind takes you. You have relinquished control over where you are going or how you are getting there. You are simply allowing yourself to be guided and directed as you repeat the words, "I am a feather on the breath of God." Unaware of your destination, you feel a sense of liberation knowing that a force bigger than yourself is in control, and you float along. This is what it feels like to let go of our ego. As you imagine yourself floating like a feather, consider the following questions: What control issues do I need to let go of in my life? What is keeping me from feeling free? When we are willing to let go of our ego, we encounter abundant grace.

O son of God, in your life you are like a field that produces both useful and vile vegetation, because through the nature of your soul, which is celestial, you delight in doing good things, but you take the vile things so much to your heart that they keep you from perfecting the good, and so, having neglected the precepts of your Creator and the promptings of our celestial soul, you more often perform those acts which your flesh demands of you. Now, therefore, let the admonition of the Holy Spirit teach you to fight manfully and untiringly in fortitude and stability.

—*Letter from Hildegard to a Lay Person*

This letter is addressed to an unnamed lay person sometime between 1173 and 1179 CE. Reflecting a common theme in Hildegard's writings, it contains spiritual advice for remaining steadfast in the face of temptation.

Reflection

Whether we consciously realize it or not, we spend an enormous amount of our lives struggling to find balance between light and darkness. Sometimes we become so overwhelmed by our tendency to do "vile things" that we lose sight of our celestial nature. It is a difficult process to acknowledge our "vile vegetation," the ways we wrong ourselves and others, but in doing so we can begin the process of transforming it into something extraordinary. We are both light and darkness, and we need to acknowledge both sides of ourselves. Think of a time when you were struggling with choices and temptations that led to grief, pain, or even shame. Reflect on how you grew through that struggle, and remember to celebrate the choices you've made that led to healing, joy, and peace.

When the mountain rises in you, your mind is like a valley, and, moreover, you think that you are constructing a city when you arrogantly condemn some matter. For who-ever applies scourges to an already festering wound brings forth poison mixed with blood. This is not productive. So it is with the mind of a person who will not, under any circum-stances, be merciful. The good physician, on the other hand, anoints the wounds.

—Letter from Hildegard to a Monk

Hildegard drew a large following from among male clergy, many of whom pledged themselves to her spiritual care. The following excerpt written sometime before 1170 CE is a response she wrote advising an unnamed monk to be compassionate and merciful to those in his care.

Reflection

Our world today is suffering from "already festering wounds" and is in dire need of the healing medicine of mercy. Hildegard beautifully defines mercy as the simple act of refraining from applying additional scourges. In dealing with ourselves and others, we must always start from a place of love and compassion from which healing will naturally follow. What wounds have you endured? In dealing with your own wounds, how can you become more like the "good physician" who compassionately anoints and heals others?

Watch over that garden which the divine gift has planted, and take care that its herbs do not wither. Rather, cut the rottenness out of them, and cast it out, for it chokes off their usefulness. In this way you will cause them to flourish. For when the sun hides its rays, the earth ceases to rejoice. And I say: Do not overshadow your garden with the weariness of silence, but in the True Light weed out those things which must be weeded out with discretion. Illuminate your temple with benevolence, and burn incense in your censer, so that its smoke may ascend to the place of the living God. And you will live forever.

—*Letter from Hildegard to Hermann,*
Bishop of Constance

This excerpt is from a second letter Hildegard wrote to Hermann, bishop of Constance, between 1148 and 1166 CE. In the first letter, she chastises him for "walking in darkness." In this letter, she again reminds him to resist the darkness and allow the Living Light to illuminate his path.

Reflection

Think of a time when you witnessed an injustice and something inside of you was compelling you to speak, yet you chose to remain silent. What prevented you from speaking your thoughts at that moment? The garden we are entrusted to care for can seem more like a wild jungle at times. Places where we would expect to be able to speak out in truth and justice, where the "weeds" should not be in control—church, school, society—are often the places with the greatest level of rottenness and overgrowth. Consider your own garden for a moment. What needs to be weeded out? Where are you being called to speak out?

The Living Light says: the Scriptures are a path which leads to the lofty mountain where flowers and precious herbs grow, a fragrant breeze blowing over them, bringing forth their sweet aroma, and where roses and lilies show their bright faces. Yet because of the shadows of dark living air, that mountain was not visible until the Son of the Most High had illuminated the world. For the Sun itself came from the dawn to illumine this mountain, and all the people saw its herbs. The day was very beautiful, and good news came into the world. But, O Shepherds, now is the time for wailing and mourning, because in our day that mountain has been overshadowed by such dark clouds that its sweet fragrance no longer is wafted down to us.

—*Letter from Hildegard to Heinrich, Bishop of Liege*

The following excerpt is from a letter Hildegard wrote to Heinrich, bishop of Liege, sometime between 1148 and 1153 CE. Heinrich wrote seeking Hildegard's guidance for overcoming his tendency to sin. She responds with great sadness at the depth of sin and darkness she perceives as present in the world.

Reflection

You are a light worker. You were created to illuminate our world through daily acts of love and justice. The task referred to as "light work" involves the act of sowing seeds of light and love in places where you find darkness and despair. The path to the lofty mountain abundant in light and grace is accessible; we need only to choose to walk to it. Though she struggled with her own sinful nature and mourned the dark clouds present in her world, Hildegard lived her life in humble service of the Living Light. Where are you being called to shine light today?

Love, which, in concert with Abstinence, establishes Faith, and which, along with Patience, builds up Chastity, is like the columns that sustain the four corners of a house. For it was that same Love which planted a glorious garden redolent with precious herbs and noble flowers—roses and lilies—which breathed forth a wondrous fragrance, that garden on which the true Solomon was accustomed to feast his eyes. . . . But, now, look to that glorious garden which love planted, and gather to yourself every virtue in true humility and simplicity of heart. And although you find yourself among men of various states of mind, learn how patient and how long-suffering divine goodness has been to us all.

—*Letter from Hildegard to the Monk Guibert*

The following is written to a monk named Guibert from Gembloux, who would become Hildegard's last secretary before she died and a key contributor to her *Vita* (medieval biography). Guibert wrote often to Hildegard asking for answers to theological questions and concerns. The following excerpt was written in 1176 CE.

Reflection

Love graces us with the vision to see the dignity inherent in every human person. In the midst of life's ongoing challenges we are called to love. Love God, love ourselves, love others, and love the whole of creation. Love does not blind us to injustice, and it is not a free pass to allow others to hurt us in mind, body, or spirit. Love empowers us to face each experience from a place of personal strength. It is the source through which the Living Light shines, without any additional effort on our part. We simply need to love. When we are rich in love, we will be rich in *viriditas*, the life force that animates all of creation. Name three things you love about yourself. Remind yourself of these things as you respond to the challenges of your day.

Now, listen again, my daughters, and hear the words of the Living Light, which has no darkness. Keep yourselves from evil things. For the whispers of the devil will come, and the whispers of many storms.... Therefore, in your minds be like one who looks at a garden where flowers and apple trees grow so that he may enjoy their aroma and eat the apples. The "aroma of apples" means a man who desires to emulate the goodness of the righteous by abstaining from sin, and "eating the apples" represents a person who faithfully governs those under his authority, and who, by the grace of God, distributes alms to the poor.... This monastery stands between two paths: one of them slimy, the other bright with sunlight.

—*Letter from Hildegard to the Congregation of Nuns*

In addition to writing to men in various political and religious places, Hildegard also wrote often to religious women. This particular excerpt is believed to have been written before 1173 CE to an unidentified community of nuns. As was her style, Hildegard used allegorical imagery to communicate her underlying message of virtue.

Reflection

Think of an experience on your journey where you had to choose which path you would take. While we often desire to take the path "bright with sunlight," we somehow find ourselves repeatedly struggling along on the "slimy" path. How does this happen? For Hildegard, everything in the created world has a proper order. When our desires are misplaced, chaos and darkness enter into our experience. We create the "slimy" paths of our lives when we take our focus off of the Light. Reflecting on your current experience, where are you currently experiencing chaos? Consider what desires may have led you there and how you can turn those desires back toward the Light.

In a vision I saw, as it were, the sun shining with excessive heat upon mud filled with worms, and these creatures stretched themselves out in joy of the heat, but, eventually not being able to bear the excessive heat, they hid themselves away, and the mud sent forth a noisome stench. I saw also that the sun shone in a garden, in which roses and lilies and all kinds of herbs grew, and the flowers grew abundantly by the heat of the sun, and the herbs sent forth innumerable roots and gave forth an exceedingly delightful odor, so that many people, suffused with this lovely fragrance, rejoiced in this garden as if it were paradise. And I heard a voice from above saying to you: Make your decision, O man, whether you wish to remain in this garden of delights or to lie with the worms in that stinking excrement.

—Letter from Hildegard to Philip,
Archbishop of Cologne

The following excerpt is from a letter Hildegard wrote to her friend Philip, archbishop of Cologne, sometime between 1170 and 1173 CE. It is the second of two letters she wrote challenging Philip to remain faithful to his office by living a virtuous life and standing strong against evil.

Reflection

Relationships can be challenging, especially when we witness a loved one heading down a path filled with "stinking excrement." We do not always have the courage to tell those we love that the path they are on is dangerous. We hesitate to speak out of fear. We are afraid we will be rejected, afraid our loved ones will be angry with us, and possibly even more afraid that our own "stinking excrement" will be brought to the light. Hildegard truly believed she was empowered by the Living Light, and this gave her strength to challenge her friend Philip when it was needed. Her words could be harsh, yet they were always written in the spirit of love. Do we seek out the presence of the Living Light, allowing ourselves not only to be warmed but to grow in our relationships? Or do we hide ourselves away, fearful of what the Light might demand of us?

In the year 1170 lying for a long time in my sickbed, fully awake in body and soul, I saw an exceedingly beautiful image of a woman. She was so delightful and so beautiful that the mind of man could never comprehend it, and in stature she reached from the earth to the heavens. Her face shone with great brightness, and with her eyes she looked into heaven. She was clothed in a garment of dazzling white silk, over which was a cloak set with precious stones—with emeralds, sapphires, and pearls—and on her feet were shoes of onyx. But her face was smudged with dirt, and her dress was torn on the right side. Moreover, her cloak had lost its exquisite beauty, and the tops of her shoes were soiled. She cried out in a loud, mournful voice to the heights of heaven.

—Letter from Hildegard to Werner

Hildegard was granted permission to go on four preaching tours. On one of her tours, she stopped at Kirchheim. She received a letter from a priest named Werner requesting a copy of her homily. This excerpt is from her response, which was written in 1170 CE.

Reflection

Life can leave us feeling battered and abused. Systematic abuse of mind, body, and spirit is so rampant that we don't always notice it is happening. We are beautiful human beings created in the image and likeness of God, dazzling and bright. Yet, years of abuse (external and self-inflicted) have caused our faces to become smudged and our clothes torn. Reflecting on Hildegard's vision, in what ways have you lost sight of the divine beauty inherent within your body, mind, and soul? Be kind to yourself and remember your value and gifts.

For God implanted the living voice of the breath of life in reason, that is, the voice of rejoicing, which by good knowledge sees and knows God by faith. The same voice is a well-sounding trumpet resonating with the works of kindness, for it enjoys the embrace of divine love, and, therefore, by means of humility gathers the meek and, with mercy, anoints their wounds. Moreover, divine love flows with the gushing water of the Holy Spirit, that is, with the peace of the goodness of God. Humility also plants a garden with every fruit-bearing tree of God's grace, which encompasses all the invigorating power of God's gifts. And mercy exudes a balm to soothe all the troubles which assail mankind.

—*Letter from Hildegard to the Five Abbots*

Hildegard wrote two major works on healing with herbs and stones. Her infirmary was well known for its extraordinary healings. As her reputation grew, her healing services were sought out by many. This particular excerpt was written sometime before 1157 CE and was a part of a much larger response to a group of five abbots requesting Hildegard heal a noble woman experiencing infertility.

Reflection

Deserts appear in various forms in the mind, body, and spirit. They are the antithesis of *viriditas* (fertility), a prevalent concept in Hildegard's thought. The symptoms we experience reflect the deep pain we carry. What a beautiful image to take to prayer: "mercy is a balm to soothe the troubles which assail mankind." Before we can begin to apply this healing elsewhere, however, we need to first heal ourselves. In what ways have you been denying the divine gifts of love and mercy to yourself? Imagine ways to practice mercy toward yourself.

O father, the Living Light has given these words to me for you: Why do you hide your face from me? You do this as if you are perturbed or angry at the mystical words which I bring forth not from myself, but as I see them in the Living Light. Indeed, things are shown to me there which my mind does not desire and which my will does not seek, but often I see them under compulsion. Therefore, I pray to God that you not consider His help as something foreign to you and that your mind may be devoted to pure knowledge so that you may gaze into the mirror of salvation. Thus you will live forever. May the bright light of God's grace never be cut off from you, but may the mercy of God protect you, so that the ancient traitor may not deceive you. Now, however, may your eye live in God, and may the viridity of your soul never dry up.

—*Letter from Hildegard to Arnold,*
Archbishop of Mainz

Hildegard lived her entire life along the Rhine Valley within the diocese of Mainz. She was in regular communication with the clerics of Mainz from the time she lived at Disibodenberg until she moved to Rupertsberg. While the relationship was rocky at times, the diocese of Mainz provided her monastery with ongoing protection, support, and

Reflection

We are never on the spiritual journey alone. We are constantly growing in relationship to God and each other through our experiences. Our path may at times feel dark and slimy, and it may seem as though we have lost our way. However, the well of Living Light, the source of *viriditas* that animates every part of the created world, is always present. As we come to the conclusion of our thirty-day journey with St. Hildegard of Bingen, may you take from this journey an increased awareness that the Living Light is within you, eager to renew the viridity of your soul. You are the presence of light in this world, and you are creating an illumined path for others by choosing peace and love. Share what you have learned on this journey as you act out of love for yourself and for those around you.

prayers, enabling her to develop into an extraordinary female leader. The following is from a letter Hildegard wrote to Arnold, the archbishop of Mainz, sometime between 1158 and 1160 CE.

Further Reading

The Letters of St. Hildegard of Bingen. Vol. 1–3. Translated by Joseph L. Baird and Radd K. Ehrman. Oxford: Oxford University Press, 1994–2004.

Jutta and Hildegard: The Biographical Sources. Translated and edited by Anna Silvas. University Park: Pennsylvania State University Press, 1999.

Scivias. Translated by Columba Hart and Jane Bishop. New York: Paulist, 1990.

Hildegard of Bingen: On Natural Philosophy and Medicine. Translated by Margret Berger. Rochester, NY: D. S. Brewer, 1999.

Hildegard of Bingen's Book of Divine Works: With Letters and Songs. Edited by Matthew Fox. Santa Fe, NM: Bear, 1987.

Hildegard of Bingen's Book of the Rewards of Life. Translated by Bruce W. Hozeski. New York: Oxford University Press, 1997.

Hildegard of Bingen: Symphonia. Translated by Barbara Newman. Ithaca, NY: Cornell University Press, 1998.

Passages

All passages come from *The Letters of Hildegard of Bingen*, vol. 1–3, trans. Joseph L. Baird and Radd K. Ehrman (Oxford: Oxford University Press, 1994–2004).

Day 1: Letter 372 Hildegard to a Certain Person, 3:158

Day 2: Letter 173r Hildegard to the Monk Heinrich, 2:132

Day 3: Letter 196 Hildegard to the Abbot Withelo, 2:171

Day 4: Letter 319 Hildegard to Bertha, Queen of the Greeks, 3:117

Day 5: Letter 156r Hildegard to the Abbess, 2:103

Day 6: Letter 234 Hildegard to Jutta, a Lay Sister, 3:33

Day 7: Letter 191r Hildegard to the Abbot, 2:158

Day 8: Letter 326 Hildegard to Countess Oda of Eberstein, 3:123

Day 9: Letter 256 Hildegard to an Abbot, 3:52

Day 10: Letter 8 Hildegard to Pope Anastasius, 1:41

Day 11: Letter 74r Hildegard to Abbot Kuno, 1:160

Day 12: Letter 370 Hildegard to a Certain Person, 3:157–58

Day 13: Letter 135 Hildegard to Abbot Manegold (?), 2:76

Day 14: Letter 279, Hildegard to Radulf, Teacher, 3:76